THE VIETNAM WAR

T0346647

THE VIETNAM WAR

Ronald B. Frankum Jr.

STACKPOLE BOOKS

Guilford, Connecticut

This book is dedicated to Jack Yuska, Jack Frey,
Bob Howe, and Gordon Rowe. Welcome home!

STACKPOLE
BOOKS

Published by Stackpole Books
An imprint of The Rowman & Littlefield Publishing Group, Inc.
4501 Forbes Blvd., Ste. 200
Lanham, MD 20706
www.rowman.com

Distributed by NATIONAL BOOK NETWORK
800-462-6420

Copyright © 2019 by Ronald B. Frankum Jr.

All rights reserved. No part of this book may be reproduced in any form or by any electronic
or mechanical means, including information storage and retrieval systems, without written
permission from the publisher, except by a reviewer who may quote passages in a review.

ISBN 978-0-8117-3664-0 (paperback)
ISBN 978-0-8117-6786-6 (e-book)

British Library Cataloguing in Publication Information available

Library of Congress Cataloging-in-Publication Data available

Library of Congress Control Number: 2019949268

♾️™ The paper used in this publication meets the minimum requirements of American National
Standard for Information Sciences—Permanence of Paper for Printed Library Materials, ANSI/
NISO Z39.48-1992.

Contents

Series Introduction

FOR MORE THAN NINETY YEARS, STACKPOLE BOOKS has been publishing the very best in military history, from ancient Rome to the modern Middle East, from foxhole to headquarters. We are proud to draw on that rich heritage—our decades of experience and expertise— in publishing this brand-new series, Battle Briefings. Intended as short overviews, these books aim to introduce readers to history's most important battles and campaigns— and, we hope, to provide a launching pad for further exploration of the endlessly fascinating nooks and crannies of military history.

What's in a Name?

The two Vietnams, created as a result of the 1954 Geneva Agreements, consisted of the Democratic Republic of Vietnam (North Vietnam), with its capital in Hanoi, and the State of Vietnam (South Vietnam), with its capital in Saigon. In October 1955, the Republic of Vietnam was proclaimed in the South.

The Vietnamese who fought the French during the First Indochina War were known as the Viet Minh, which was an abbreviation for the Viet Nam Doc Lap Dong Minh Hoi, or League for the Independence of Vietnam. This group disbanded in 1951, though the name lingered in American circles until the end of the 1950s, when the organization was renamed the Viet Cong (Cong San Viet Nam) by South Vietnamese president Ngo Dinh Diem to link the group to the Communist North. These insurgents, however, called themselves the Mat Tran Dan Toc Giai Phong Mien Nam Viet Nam (National Front for the Liberation of South Vietnam, or NLF).

For consistency and ease in understanding this complex war, the terms *North Vietnam*, *South Vietnam*, *Viet Minh*, and *Viet Cong* are used. ■

Introduction

THERE ARE SEVERAL POTENTIAL points of origin for the start of the Vietnam War. From a Vietnamese perspective, the struggle to gain identity and independence has its origins before the start of the first century, and there were several moments in Vietnam's first one thousand years that hold significance for the Vietnamese in their crusade. From the American perspective, the origins are simpler to identify, but even so, there is controversy. President Woodrow Wilson's neglect of Ho Chi Minh's appeal for Vietnamese self-determination at Versailles at the end of the First World War might be thought of as the start of the modern war. However, it seems more reasonable to begin with the events of the Second World War and the American efforts against the Japanese in the Pacific theater. This was a time when the United States had an opportunity to effect change in Southeast Asia.

During this war, President Franklin D. Roosevelt had made it clear that colonialism was nearing its end. Roosevelt believed Indochina, an area created and controlled by the French since the 1880s, should be transformed into an independent state, or series of states, through the process of an international trusteeship. Roosevelt argued that the French had lost their claim on the people of Indochina through their failed colonial experiment, which had lasted more than eighty years. He did not think the French had earned another chance to reconstitute their colonial past based on their actions during the Second World War. Roosevelt argued for a more global perspective in American

Ho Chi Minh during a visit to Poland, 1957. INP PC 1348728, 57-17488, NATIONAL ARCHIVES AND RECORDS ADMINISTRATION, COLLEGE PARK, MD.

ix

foreign policy in the postwar period, where the United States would aid in the transition of former colonies into contributing members of an international community. His death on April 12, 1945, and the ascension of Vice President Harry S. Truman to the presidency altered these plans.

Unlike Roosevelt, Truman had a more Eurocentric view of the world. He believed that the next world war would be in Europe rather than in the former colonies. As such, Truman maintained that the United States needed a strong France to counter potential Communist encroachment into Western Europe. This new direction in American foreign policy meant that the transformation of Indochina no longer was a priority for the United States. In its efforts to contain Communism in Europe, the Truman administration authorized a series of efforts that helped to entrench a cold war mentality in the United States in which any gain for the Communist world was considered a loss for the West, regardless of the circumstances surrounding that event. Because Truman had tied Europe's fate to France and the French insisted that its future was dependent upon its colonial possessions, Truman began the process of supporting the French effort to retain Indochina.

President Dwight D. Eisenhower and Secretary of State John Foster Dulles greet Ngo Dinh Diem, May 8, 1957. 342-AF-18302AF, NATIONAL ARCHIVES AND RECORDS ADMINISTRATION, COLLEGE PARK, MD.

Timeline of Cold War Events (1945–1950)

February 22, 1946:	George Kennan's "long telegram," written from the American embassy in Moscow, suggests that the United States could never negotiate with the Soviet Union, whose Communist ideology was formed from a "neurotic view of world affairs" and an "instinctive Russian sense of insecurity"
March 5, 1946:	Former British prime minister Winston Churchill delivers his "Iron Curtain" speech in Fulton, Missouri, during which he proclaims that the United States stands "at this time at the pinnacle of world power" and warns that due to Soviet action "an iron curtain has descended across the Continent"
June 5, 1947:	During his Harvard University commencement speech, Secretary of State George C. Marshall announces an economic plan to rebuild Europe, which becomes known as the Marshall Plan
July 1947:	George Kennan's "Mr. X" article in *Foreign Affairs*, titled "The Sources of Soviet Conduct," argues that the United States must adopt a "policy of firm containment" to confront the aggressive Soviet Union
July 1947:	The National Security Act creates the Department of Defense, the National Security Council (NSC), and the Central Intelligence Agency
June 1948– May 1949:	Berlin Blockade
April 4, 1949:	North Atlantic Treaty Organization is formed
August 29, 1949:	Soviet Union tests its first atomic bomb
October 1949:	Creation of the People's Republic of China (fall of China)
April 1950:	National Security Council Paper Number 68 (NSC-68) predicts prolonged global tension with Soviet military expansion and a need to unite the free world in defense of democracy
June 1950– July 1953:	Korean War

FIRST INDOCHINA WAR

At the end of the Second World War in 1945, the leader of the Viet Minh, Ho Chi Minh, established the Democratic Republic of Vietnam as the first step in declaring Vietnam's independence from France. However, Ho Chi Minh and his negotiators failed to reach an agreement with the French and, on December 19, 1946, attacked French forces in Hanoi. This signaled the start of the First Indochina War, which would last until the French defeat at Dien Bien Phu in May 1954. During this time, the United States supported the French effort to defeat the Vietnamese despite Roosevelt's earlier indication that the French no longer deserved a place in Indochina.

The United States was not actively involved in the First Indochina War. Instead, it took a more passive approach by providing the French with military hardware and financial support. On February 7, 1950, Truman ordered his National Security Council (NSC) to create a policy for the American role in Southeast Asia. NSC 64, approved in March 1950, added Indochina to the United States' Cold War battle against Communism and served as the foundation for America's twenty-five-year involvement in Vietnam.

1

The document also established an American military presence in Indochina with the formation of the Military Assistance Advisory Group (MAAG), Indochina, whose personnel began to arrive in Saigon in September 1950.

Despite American support for the French and its allies in Indochina, the Vietnamese resistance was able to wear down its enemy in a prolonged guerrilla-style war. As France became more disenchanted with the war in Indochina, the US aid to its ally increased. By the end of 1953, the United States was providing a significant portion of the financial burden without an end in sight. This led to the development of a French strategy named after the commander of the French Union Forces in Indochina, General Henri Navarre. The Navarre Plan called for a consolidation of French Union

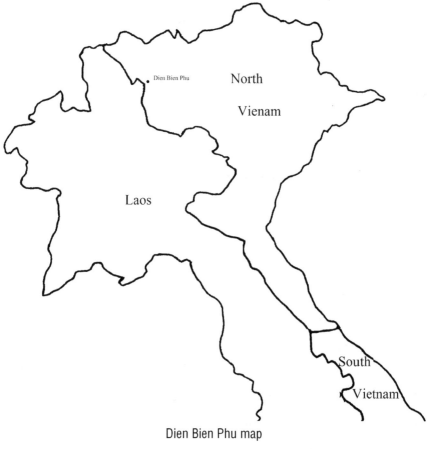

Dien Bien Phu map

forces in the North and then a series of strikes against the Vietnamese insurgents led by Vo Nguyen Giap to isolate and destroy this threat. The Vietnamese thwarted this plan and forced Navarre to revise his strategy. He chose to concentrate a significant number of his northern forces near the village of Dien Bien Phu. The French built up a series of strongholds that threatened the Vietnamese ability to move along the strategic Route 19 between Laos and North Vietnam. By forcing the Vietnamese to confront this threat, Navarre hoped that superior French artillery and airpower could decimate the concentrated Vietnamese forces. The French, however, underestimated the ability of the Vietnamese to adapt to the conditions around Dien Bien Phu and became the victims of their own trap. The French fortress of Dien Bien Phu fell on May 7, 1954, a day before a planned conference in Geneva, Switzerland, took up the issue of the war in Indochina.

The military failure at Dien Bien Phu signaled the end of French colonial rule in Indochina. The 1954 Geneva Agreements established the parameters for the transfer of power to the Vietnamese. However, representatives of the United States and the State of Vietnam, an area that consisted of the southern half of the country, refused to sign the document. The United States declared that it would respect the integrity of the agreement so long as all signatories did the same, while Ngo Dinh Diem, the leader and representative of Vietnamese emperor Bao Dai, argued that the Communist North would not respect the agreements in their efforts to reunite the country under their own rule. As a result, the Geneva Agreements failed to end the conflict in Vietnam even though the French no longer had a significant presence in the country.

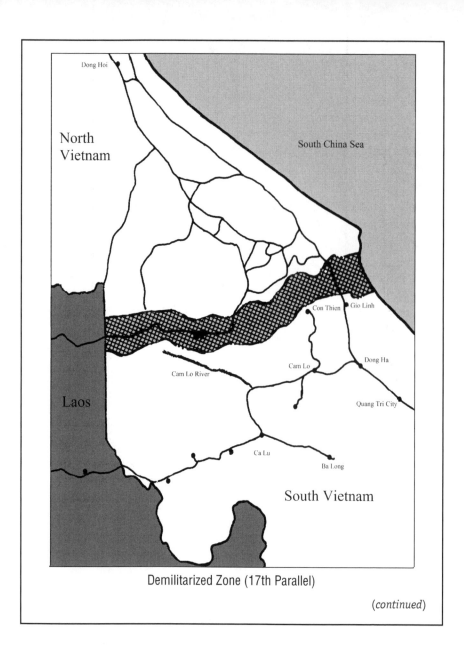

Dong Hoi

North
Vietnam

South China Sea

Con Thien   Gio Linh

Cam Lo   Dong Ha

Cam Lo River

Laos

Quang Tri City

Ca Lu

Ba Long

South Vietnam

Demilitarized Zone (17th Parallel)

(continued)

American Response to the Geneva Agreements Submitted to the Eighth Plenary Session on Indochina, Geneva, July 21, 1954

The Government of the United States being resolved to devote its efforts to the strengthening of peace in accordance with the principles and purposes of the United Nations takes note of the agreements concluded at Geneva on July 20 and 21, 1954 between the (a) Franco-Laotian command and the command of the Peoples Army of VietNam; (b) the Royal Khmer Army Command and the command of the Peoples Army of Viet-Nam; (c) Franco-Vietnamese command and the command of the Peoples Army of Vietnam and of paragraphs 1 to 12 inclusive of the declaration presented to the Geneva Conference on July 21, 1954 declares with regard to the aforesaid agreements and paragraphs that (i) it will refrain from the threat or the use of force to disturb them, in accordance with Article 2 (4) of the Charter of the United Nations dealing with the obligation of members to refrain in their international relations from the threat or use of force; and (ii) it will view any renewal of the aggression in violation of the aforesaid agreements with grave concern and as seriously threatening international peace and security. ∎

(Source: Editorial Note, *Foreign Relations of the United States, 1952–1954, Indochina*, Volume XIII, Part 2, Document 1073.)

CHAPTER 2

NATION BUILDING

The end of the First Indochina War did not bring a period of peace and calm for Vietnam. After the Geneva Agreements, the State of Vietnam under-went a series of challenges that tested not only that country but also the United States. One stipulation of the Geneva Agreements was the free movement of people between the two Vietnams for a period of three hundred days. This resulted in a mass exodus of Vietnamese from the North who fled because of fear of retribution for their support of the French in the First Indochina War or their religion as well as individuals who believed they had a better chance in the South. The refugee crisis, which eventually involved the relocation of more than 810,000 people, overwhelmed the Vietnamese and French. On August 8, 1954, the United States Navy agreed to assist in the movement of individuals in what became known as Operation Passage to Freedom. The ten-month mission saw the movement of 310,000 Vietnamese aboard US ships. The interaction between Vietnamese and US sailors also established a foundation of trust and obligation upon which

Roger K. Ackley, USOM (Special Technical and Economic Mission) to Cambodia, Laos, and Vietnam:

What would happen if southern Vietnam fell? Of course it is our policy to do everything in our power to be sure it does not fall, and, true enough, the situation is improving, but what if it does fall. I am convinced that morally as well as politically, we are bound to take steps to assist as many as possible in whatever time is permitted to avoid fearful retribution at the hands of the Communists. Be it right or wrong, we have declared ourselves to these people and to the world as encouraging their flight to freedom, and, participating in it. We have therefore, morally married a long term responsibility. Even politically, we must not lose face in the Far East by selling these people short. ∎

(Source: Roger Ackley, "Subject-Escapee Planning in Vietnam," February 22, 1954, Folder 7, "Weekly-Haiphong, 1954–1955," Box 5, Series 1455 "Resettlement and Rehabilitation Division, Field Service, Classified Subject Files, 1954–1958," RG 469 "Records of the Agency for International Development and Predecessor Agencies," National Archives and Records Administration, College Park, MD.)

VA000873, DOUGLAS PIKE PHOTOGRAPH COLLECTION, THE VIETNAM CENTER AND ARCHIVE, TEXAS TECH UNIVERSITY.

many within the United States based their decisions for the remainder of the decade.

If the United States was fully committed to the Vietnamese refugee crisis, it was less involved in the early political struggles of Ngo Dinh Diem and his consolidation of power in the South. The influx of refugees from the North and competing factions in the South, some still linked to the French, created a climate of instability. American officials seemed content to see which group survived before fully committing. While the country was led by Emperor Bao Dai, the real power and Vietnam's best hope rested with Ngo Dinh Diem, whose forces would eventually defeat the combined threat of the three political-religious sects, the Cao Dai, Hoa Hao, and Binh Xuyen, which also vied for power and control of the country. With his victory and proclamation of the Republic of Vietnam in October 1955, Ngo Dinh Diem became the key Vietnamese leader for American plans in Southeast Asia. However, he was less accommodating than the United States would have liked.

Although Ngo Dinh Diem and American officials in South Vietnam had the same objectives, the means by which these goals were to be achieved differed. American military officials, such as MAAG commander General Samuel Williams and his successor General Lionel McGarr, were able to work with Ngo Dinh Diem much better than members of the American diplomatic corps. Of particular concern was the relationship between the Vietnamese president and the US ambassador, Elbridge Durbrow.

When Durbrow first arrived in Vietnam in 1957, he was favorably impressed with the progress that Ngo Dinh Diem had made. At the end of his four-year tenure, however, Durbrow actively advocated the removal of Ngo Dinh Diem, indirectly supported a November 1960 attempted coup d'état through inaction, and became involved in the political intrigue that dominated Saigon. As a result, and despite the good rapport with the US military, the relationship between the Vietnamese and the Americans was tense as John F. Kennedy entered the White House in 1961.

Discontent in South Vietnam

Discontent with President Ngo Dinh Diem's continuing dictatorial rule is a potential threat to the stability of the South Vietnamese Government. Criticism of Diem's authoritarianism is being heard increasingly among influential Vietnamese, including members of his own cabinet, who formerly supported the President unswervingly.

Diem is isolated from the public by his dependence on a tight circle of advisers, headed by his brother Ngo Dinh Nhu. Nhu, who is widely feared and hated, also heads the elite Can Lao party, which controls all political activity in Vietnam. The police-state methods of the Can Lao and the activities of its covert branches have caused much resentment within the government.

[Section redacted]

Saigon's preoccupation with internal security to the detriment of economic progress, coupled with heavy-handed police measures, is also engendering resentment among the masses. This plays into the hands of the Vietnamese Communists who appear to be stepping up their clandestine activities aimed at toppling Diem.

[Section redacted] ■

(Source: Daily Briefing, "Discontent in South Vietnam," October 1, 1958, Current Intelligence Bulletin, Central Intelligence Agency, Office of Current Intelligence, Declassified Documents, National Archives and Records Administration, College Park, MD.)

A Viet Cong soldier crouches in a bunker with an SKS rifle, 1968. DENNIS J. KURPUIS, SPC4, 111-CC-53045, NARA. ▶

CHAPTER 3

KENNEDY ADMINISTRATION

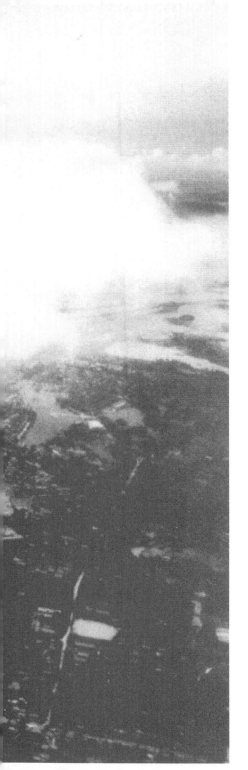

The situation in Southeast Asia took on a prominent role within the Kennedy administration in its opening days. While the initial concern focused on Laos, which was under threat from a Communist insurgency known as the Pathet Lao, Vietnam soon overshadowed its neighbor. During his first year, Kennedy authorized numerous escalatory measures in South Vietnam that shifted the focus from the Eisenhower administration strategy of nation building toward one that committed American prestige and power to its embattled ally. Kennedy sought to reestablish a more friendly relationship with Ngo Dinh Diem by replacing Durbrow with Frederick Nolting. The Kennedy administration increased the number of American advisers in Vietnam; created the Military Assistance Command, Vietnam (MACV), to replace the MAAG; and offered more sophisticated weapons to the Army of the Republic of Vietnam (ARVN). It also sustained a public relations campaign that both promised continued support for the Vietnamese and warned the Communist nations that the United States would not stand by and allow Southeast Asia to fall to Communism.

President John F. Kennedy, July 25, 1961. WHITE HOUSE/6712-D, 61-12622, NATIONAL ARCHIVES AND RECORDS ADMINISTRATION, COLLEGE PARK, MD.

L et every nation know, whether it wishes us well or ill, that we shall pay any price, bear any burden, meet any hardship, support any friend, oppose any foe to assure the survival and the success of liberty. . . .

To those new states whom we welcome to the ranks of the free, we pledge our word that one form of colonial control shall not have passed away merely to be replaced by a far more iron tyranny. We shall not always expect to find them supporting our view. But we shall always hope to find them strongly supporting their own freedom—and to remember that, in the past, those who foolishly sought power by riding the back of the tiger ended up inside.

To those people in the huts and villages of half the globe struggling to break the bonds of mass misery, we pledge our best efforts to help them help themselves, for whatever period is required—not because the communists may be doing it, not because we seek their votes, but because it is right. If a free society cannot help the many who are poor, it cannot save the few who are rich. ■

Despite increased American support for Vietnam, the Communist insurgency known as the Viet Cong continued to gain ground. One of the principal objectives for both sides was control of the Vietnamese people. Ngo Dinh Diem's forces kept the cities relatively secure, but thousands of hamlets in the countryside were the victims of terror, neglect, and intimidation in an attempt to control the people. The Viet Cong combined fear and brutality with propaganda and positive actions to destabilize the population. The Republic of Vietnam was forced to react to these efforts by attempting a series of measures designed to protect the people and eliminate the insurgency's presence. Vietnamese government answers to these dilemmas, such as the Agroville Program (1959–1961), which resettled large numbers of Vietnamese peasants into protected centers, and the Strategic Hamlet Program (1962–1964), which attempted a more nuanced approach to accomplish its goals, failed to alleviate the suffering of the people.

The interactions between the Americans involved in these programs with Ngo Dinh Diem, and his brother Ngo Dinh Nhu, who was intimately involved in each effort, strained the relationship between the two nations. There were many within the Kennedy administration who believed that Ngo Dinh Diem had outlasted his usefulness to US strategy in Southeast Asia. Continued setbacks in Vietnam and a growing frustration among American officials involved in that country set the stage for significant changes in 1963.

The year 1963 started off poorly for South Vietnam. On January 2, the ARVN's 7th Division suffered a defeat at the hands of the Viet Cong near the village of Ap Bac. The engagement reinforced the fear that the Vietnamese were not as developed militarily, despite increased US assistance. It also called into question the military's reporting of the battle after MACV commander, General Paul Harkins, declared that the operation was successful even though American journalists who arrived on the scene the next day received a different story. In addition to this military setback, the internal stability in Vietnam suffered due to a Buddhist uprising that summer. The crisis began with

Memorandum of a Conversation between President Kennedy and Assistant Secretary of State for Far Eastern Affairs, Averell Harriman, White House, Washington, D.C., April 6, 1962

The Governor [Harriman] said that while he thought that Diem was a losing horse in the long run, he did not think we should actively work against him, because there was nobody to replace him. Rather our policy should be to support the government and people of Viet-Nam, rather than Diem personally. ∎

(Source: *Foreign Relations of the United States, 1961–1963, Volume II, Vietnam, 1962*: 309.)

Vietnamese youth take positions for hamlet defense drill. USIA/SAIGON (62-18521), 66-1545, NATIONAL ARCHIVES AND RECORDS ADMINISTRATION, COLLEGE PARK, MD.

Ngo Dinh Diem refusing to allow the flying of the Buddhist flag as part of a celebration to mark the birth of Buddha, citing a law that prohibited the flying of any flag other than the Republic of Vietnam. This law had earlier been ignored when the Catholic flag was prominently displayed during the silver jubilee for Archbishop Ngo Dinh Thuc, the brother of the president. When Buddhists demonstrated against this inconsistency, local security forces attacked the protestors, killing nine. Tension and protests intensified and included

acts of Buddhist monk self-immolation in opposition to Ngo Dinh Diem's continued rule. These events, coupled with the deteriorating conditions of the Strategic Hamlet program and another switch of US ambassadors, culminated in the American decision to stop backing Ngo Dinh Diem.

On November 1, 1963, elements of the Vietnam military and dissenting politicians conducted a successful coup d'état against Ngo Dinh Diem. Learning from their earlier mistakes in the failed November 1960 attempt, the coup d'état

US Ambassadors to the Republic of Vietnam	
Donald R. Heath	(1952–1955)
G. Frederick Reinhardt	(1955–1957)
Elbridge Durbrow	(1957–1961)
Frederick Nolting	(1961–1963)
Henry Cabot Lodge Jr.	(1963–1964)
Maxwell D. Taylor	(1964–1965)
Henry Cabot Lodge Jr.	(1965–1967)
Ellsworth Bunker	(1967–1973)
Graham A. Martin	(1973–1975)

during which various factions, which Ngo Dinh Diem had been able to keep under control, vied for power. It was not until Nguyen Van Thieu and Nguyen Cao Ky formed an uneasy alliance in 1965 that the Republic of Vietnam achieved the kind of stability it had seen under Ngo Dinh Diem. Johnson entered the White House at a critical time for Vietnam. The US Vietnam policy was in disarray, and the prospects for a peaceful resolution were remote. Several key events that occurred in 1964 forced the United States further down the road started by the Kennedy administration. These events would eventually introduce American combat troops into Vietnam.

Johnson made it clear that the United States remained committed to its ally and would act accordingly to ensure that Vietnam was protected against Communism. In many respects, Johnson honored the Kennedy administration's policies in Vietnam, as he sought to secure the former president's legacy in social justice. It was the failure to reconcile these dueling objectives that ultimately identified the Vietnam War with Lyndon Johnson.

The process by which the United States assumed control over the war in Vietnam was a long affair. Throughout 1964, Viet Cong soldiers, who were being supported

participants captured and executed Ngo Dinh Diem and his brother Ngo Dinh Nhu before they could rally support to their side. Neither the United States nor the Republic of Vietnam had time to fully realize the significance of this event before another shook the foundation of the alliance. On November 22, Kennedy was assassinated in Dallas, Texas. These two events signaled a major shift in American diplomacy in Southeast Asia. Vice President Lyndon Baines Johnson assumed the presidency while Vietnam underwent a tumultuous period

Vice President Hubert Humphrey (center) with Chief of State Nguyen Van Thieu (left) and Prime Minister Nguyen Cao Ky (right), February 10, 1966. JUSPAO/SAIGON, 66-890, NATIONAL ARCHIVES AND RECORDS ADMINISTRATION, COLLEGE PARK, MD.

and supplemented by military units from North Vietnam, became brasher in their attacks against ARVN units as well as American advisers serving in Vietnam. Such incidents included the May 2 attack against the USS *Card*, which was docked in Saigon harbor, and the July 6 attack against the Nam Dong base. Both episodes resulted in American casualties. The United States did not respond to these provocations until the August 2 attack by North Vietnamese torpedo boats against the USS *Maddox*, which was conducting an electronic intelligence mission in the Gulf of Tonkin. A second alleged attack occurred on August 4, which prompted the Johnson administration to order a retaliatory air strike from two aircraft carriers stationed nearby. The Johnson administration responded to these attacks by pushing through Congress a resolution that would allow the US military to protect its assets in Southeast Asia. On August 7, the Senate and House of Representatives approved Joint Resolution of Congress H.J. Res. 1145, which became known as the Gulf of Tonkin Resolution. Johnson would use the resolution

Gulf of Tonkin Resolution

(H. J. Resolution 1145, August 7, 1964)

To promote the maintenance of international peace and security in southeast Asia.

Whereas naval units of the Communist regime in Vietnam, in violation of the principles of the Charter of the United Nations and of international law, have deliberately and repeatedly attacked United States naval vessels lawfully present in international waters, and have thereby created a serious threat to international peace; and

Whereas these attackers are part of deliberate and systematic campaign of aggression that the Communist regime in North Vietnam has been waging against its neighbors and the nations joined with them in the collective defense of their freedom; and

Whereas the United States is assisting the peoples of southeast Asia to protest their freedom and has no territorial, military or political ambitions in that area, but desires only that these people should be left in peace to work out their destinies in their own way: Now, therefore be it

Resolved by the Senate and House of Representatives of the United States of America in Congress assembled, That the Congress approves and supports the determination of the President, as Commander in Chief, to take all necessary measures to repel any armed attack against the forces of the United States and to prevent further aggression.

Section 2. The United States regards as vital to its national interest and to world peace the maintenance of international peace and security in southeast Asia. Consonant with the Constitution of the United States and the Charter of the United Nations and in accordance with its obligations under the Southeast Asia Collective Defense Treaty, the United States is, therefore, prepared, as the President determines, to take all necessary steps, including the use of armed force, to assist any member or protocol state of the Southeast Asia Collective Defense Treaty requesting assistance in defense of its freedom.

Section 3. This resolution shall expire when the President shall determine that the peace and security of the area is reasonably assured by international conditions created by action of the United Nations or otherwise, except that it may be terminated earlier by concurrent resolution of the Congress. ■

(Source: Department of State Bulletin, August 25, 1964: 268.)

to claim American support for his administration's decisions in Vietnam as the war intensified.

The Johnson administration also approved of a retaliatory air strike against North Vietnam. Operation Pierce Arrow was the first of many US air campaigns in Southeast Asia. Additional attacks and reprisals occurred for the rest of 1964, but Johnson, who was engaged in a presidential election against Arizona senator Barry Goldwater, chose to minimize the publicity of American action and escalation in Southeast Asia. This escalation included additional advisers, military assistance, and a widening of the air war in the southern portion of Laos, which was being used by the North Vietnamese to move personnel and material down what became known as the Ho Chi Minh Trail.

After the November election, in which Johnson won a decisive victory, Vietnam again demanded American attention. On December 28, the Viet Cong overwhelmed the garrison at Binh Gia and then defeated two companies of ARVN troops sent to relieve the besieged village. Additional army units and marines arrived over the next two days and engaged in heavy fighting against a reinforced Viet Cong unit. The Vietnamese military suffered four hundred men killed, wounded, or missing. This battle reinforced the American military perception that the Vietnamese were no match for their enemy. The other events of 1964 coupled with this military defeat hastened the decision of the United States to increase its presence in Southeast Asia in order to ensure the survival of the Republic of Vietnam.

On February 7, 1965, Viet Cong forces mortared Camp Holloway, an American base near Pleiku in the Central Highlands. The attack killed eight Americans and wounded more than one hundred others, as well as destroying several helicopters and fixed-wing aircraft. In response, the Johnson administration authorized a retaliatory airstrike, with the operational name Flaming Dart. The purpose of the operation was to target North Vietnamese facilities that potentially could have supported the February 7 attack. Undeterred, the Viet Cong countered by attacking the American billet in Qui Nhon on February 10, killing twenty-three personnel. The United States responded with a second round of Flaming Dart missions, which included both US and South Vietnamese aircraft.

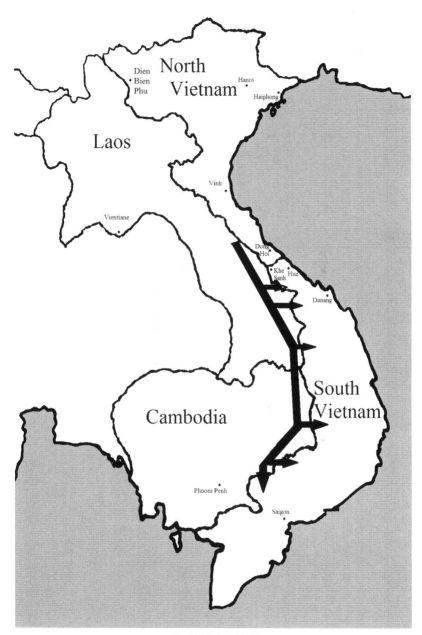

Ho Chi Minh Trail

CHAPTER 4

AMERICANIZATION OF THE VIETNAM WAR

In response to the two attacks and in anticipation of further involvement to stem the deteriorating conditions in the South, the Johnson administration developed an eight-week air campaign with the primary purpose of stopping the infiltration of North Vietnamese personnel and supplies into the Republic of Vietnam. Initiated on March 2, 1965, the operation, known as Rolling Thunder, extended beyond the eight-week program and became one of the most significant air campaigns of the war. It coincided with the decision to introduce US combat troops into strategic areas. The purpose of this "enclave strategy" was to protect the major cities and military bases as well as the physical assets used to support the air operation. The enclave strategy was more defensive in nature and relied upon the ARVN to take the offensive against the enemy combatants operating in the countryside. The strategy received the endorsement of the American ambassador, Maxwell Taylor, though the MACV commander, General William Westmoreland, advocated a more aggressive approach with the American forces under his command.

Operation Rolling Thunder

Operation Rolling Thunder began on March 2, 1965, and was originally conceived as an eight-week air campaign designed to react to North Vietnamese and Viet Cong activities in South Vietnam. With the escalation of American involvement, the air operation took on a new role and was extended beyond its original limited scope. Rolling Thunder sorties were used to hinder the ability of the North Vietnamese to move personnel and supplies into South Vietnam, attack targets of opportunity, and damage the military infrastructure in the North. While the air campaign did achieve some success, it was not enough to dissuade Hanoi from continuing with its efforts to destabilize the Saigon government, nor was it a factor in forcing North Vietnam to negotiate a peaceful resolution to the war.

The restrictive nature of the air operation limited its overall effectiveness, as the United States sought to limit international condemnation of its air attacks and lessen the possibility of justification for escalatory actions by North Vietnamese allies. By 1968, Rolling Thunder had served its useful purpose, although it had failed to achieve its original goals. On March 31, the Johnson administration focused Rolling Thunder sorties on interdiction above the Demilitarized Zone and eventually ended the air campaign on November 1 in an effort to boost the fledgling presidential campaign of Democrat Hubert Humphrey. ■

Bombing of North Vietnam oil depots, July 1, 1966. UNITED STATES NAVY, 66-2347, NATIONAL ARCHIVES AND RECORDS ADMINISTRATION, COLLEGE PARK, MD.

Westmoreland requested an additional forty-four battalions of American and allied troops so that he could not only protect the vulnerable areas but also conduct operations designed to seek out and kill the enemy.

As 1965 progressed, the number of American combat troops increased. With this burgeoning force, Westmoreland authorized a series of operations, more commonly known as search-and-destroy missions, to decrease the North Vietnamese and Viet Cong threat. An early marine operation, titled Starlite, highlighted the difficulties the United States would face in the years to come as the Viet Cong and North Vietnamese, who operated more efficiently in the diverse topography and climate of Vietnam, eluded major engagements and controlled the level of intensity on the battlefield. On August 18, members of the 3rd Battalion, 3rd Marines made an amphibious landing near the suspected headquarters of a Viet Cong battalion at Van Tuong in the northern part of South Vietnam. The marines made sporadic contact with the Viet Cong throughout the day but failed to engage the enemy on their own terms. When there was fighting, the marines successfully completed some of the

Selected List of Major US Military Operations (1965–1967)

1965
Starlite (August)

Shining Brass (September)

Piranha (September)

Silver Bayonet (November)

Blue Marlin (November)

Harvest Moon (December)

1966
Masher/White Wing
    (January–March)

Double Eagle I (January–February)

Double Eagle II (February)

Abilene (March–April)

Deckhouse (June–March 1967)

Attleboro (September–November)

Thayer (September)

Irving (October)

1967
Cedar Falls (January)

Junction City (February–May)

Union (April–May)

Union II (May–June)

objectives of the search-and-destroy missions, but by the end of the operation, the Viet Cong battalion remained a presence in the region.

This type of operation was repeated several times throughout the remainder of 1965 and into 1966 and 1967. These search-and-destroy missions supported the strategy of attrition. Attrition, the process of killing more of the enemy than they could bring into battle, was fraught with difficulties, as the nature of the fighting in Vietnam sometimes made it impossible to determine how many of the enemy were actually killed or wounded.

The first large-scale battle between American and North Vietnamese forces occurred in the Ia Drang Valley in November 1965 during Operation Silver Bayonet. The 1st Battalion, 7th Cavalry engaged with a North Vietnamese division on November 14 that decided to fight rather than avoid the American force. The North Vietnamese conducted a series of frontal assaults against 7th Cavalry positions throughout the day and night and continued to attack even after the 2nd Battalion of the 7th Cavalry arrived as reinforcement. When it appeared that the North Vietnamese would overrun the American position, the commander in the field, Colonel Hal Moore,

called in airstrikes and artillery on American positions where the North Vietnamese had infiltrated. Fighting continued through November 16. The United States lost 85 killed in action and 121 wounded. During the extraction of troops on November 17 from a landing zone away from the main battle, North Vietnamese forces ambushed the 2nd Battalion, 7th Cavalry and 2nd Battalion, 5th Cavalry, which had joined the fighting earlier. The result was an additional 155 killed in action or missing and 124 wounded. The Battle for the Ia Drang Valley resulted in the largest number of American casualties to date. It brought the realities of the Vietnam War home to Americans and reinforced the notion that US involvement in the conflict would not be short or without casualties.

The United States and South Vietnam were not alone in fighting the Viet Cong and North Vietnamese. Several nations under the "Show the Flag" program allied themselves with the South. These Third Country forces participated in such operations as Abilene, during which the 1st Battalion of the Royal Australian Regiment and the 161st New Zealand Artillery joined elements of the 1st Division and 173rd Airborne Brigade in a search-and-destroy mission east

◀ Marines on patrol, January 28, 1966. K. HENDERSON, LCPL, 127-N-A186578, NARA.

Third Country Forces

On April 13, 1964, President Johnson proposed a plan that called for other nations to engage in Vietnam to help stop the spread of Communism. The plan, known as the Show the Flag or Many Flags program, was designed to ease international and domestic criticism of increased US involvement in Southeast Asia while at the same time demonstrating to North Vietnam that the free world was united against its aggressiveness. While the program could boast a greater number and percentage of Third Country Forces (personnel not originating from South Vietnam or the United States) than what was contributed by United Nations forces during the Korean War, it failed to achieve either of its objectives.

Major contributors of troops included the Republic of Korea, Australia, New Zealand, Thailand, and the Philippines. Korean participation significantly eclipsed all other countries, but its propaganda value was diminished by instances of alleged brutality and by the fact that the United States paid for the Korean troops in Vietnam. While Australia paid its own way, its three-battalion commitment made up too small a percentage of the troops fighting the North Vietnamese and Viet Cong to gain a propaganda victory. At its peak in 1968, more than sixty-eight thousand allied forces were in Southeast Asia. The United States pointed to forty-three countries that had contributed to the Saigon government, although many of these nations offered only one-time gifts, and few provided significant financial or material donations. ■

of Saigon and Operation Irving. During this mission, Korean troops joined ARVN and members of the 1st Air Cavalry Division in an attempt to eliminate the North Vietnamese threat along the coast in Binh Dinh province. By the end of 1965, there were more than 180,000 US personnel in the Republic of Vietnam. That number would double by the end of 1966. As American forces assumed a greater share of the burden in defending the Saigon government, domestic concerns increased in the United States.

The Growing Anti-War Movement

The anti-war movement against American involvement in Southeast Asia can trace its origins to the 1950s. These individuals and organizations protested all aspects of what they perceived to be aggres-

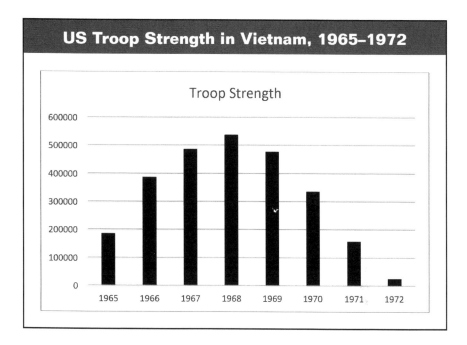

US Troop Strength in Vietnam, 1965–1972

Troop Strength

sive US action, not the events in Vietnam. The 1950s protest organizations included the Fellowship of Reconciliation and the War Resisters League. These groups questioned the use of American personnel and dollars in Southeast Asia under the guise of a Cold War strategy and believed the United States needed to acknowledge the indigenous nature of the conflict. Criticism of American action in Vietnam intensified during the Kennedy administration, more in regard to the continued American support of Ngo Dinh Diem than the escalatory actions of the United States.

By 1963, with the failures at Ap Bac and the Buddhist Crisis,

members of the media had joined in the condemnation of some of the activities but still supported the anti-Communist mission of the American presence. It was not until after the Gulf of Tonkin incident that a more organized anti-war movement surfaced within the United States. Led by individuals such as Phillip Berrigan, who founded the Emergency Citizens' Group Concerned about Vietnam and cofounded (with his brother David) the Catholic Peace Fellowship, as well as longtime pacifist A. J. Muste, who organized the Fellowship of Reconciliation in anti-war demonstrations in October 1964, these early efforts to

Marines on patrol near Danang, 1965. SERGEANT D.E. KRAMER, 127-N-A193157, NARA.

spearhead protests received little public support.

It was not until after the announcement of Operation Rolling Thunder and the insertion of marines at Danang in March 1965 that the anti-war movement gained momentum. The Students for a Democratic Society (SDS), led by Tom Hayden, assumed leadership in the movement by helping to organize teach-ins at major universities to educate the student population about Vietnam and sponsored "We Won't Go" petitions for draft-eligible men. The first teach-in, modeled after the civil rights sit-ins of the early 1960s, occurred at the Uni-versity of Michigan, Ann Arbor, on March 24 with approximately twenty-five hundred individuals involved. Other universities followed this model; on May 21, an event organized at the University of California, Berkeley, included nearly thirty thousand people. The SDS also organized a demonstration against the war in Washington, D.C., in April that brought twenty thousand participants to the nation's capital.

In August, the National Coordinating Committee to End the War in Vietnam was established with the purpose of coordinating the many anti-war organizations that had originated in 1965. It also

AMERICANIZATION OF THE VIETNAM WAR

sought to advance the movement to the national level. The Committee helped organize the October 15–16 International Days of Protest, designed to educate and disseminate information on the anti-war movement. By the end of 1965, student groups had been joined by other mainstream elements within the population. American clergy organized two groups in 1966 to unite its membership against the war. The National Emergency Committee and the Clergy Concerned about Vietnam (which was later renamed the National Emergency Committee of Clergy and Laymen Concerned about Vietnam) both had the effect

Marines walking through punji-stake defenses, January 28, 1966. K. HENDERSON, LCPL, 127-N-A186578, NARA.

Operation Hawthorne, June 7, 1966. SERGEANT BERNIE MANGIBOYAT, 111-CC-35682, NARA.

of legitimizing the growing opposition to the Vietnam War.

By 1967, another organization, the Spring Mobilization to End the War in Vietnam, formed in order to coordinate mass protests against US involvement in Southeast Asia. Its first national event, an April 25 demonstration, brought more than two hundred thousand people together throughout the United States in protest. Restructured under the National Mobilization Committee to End

Operation Hastings, July 1966. FINNELL, 127-N-A187266, NARA.

Operation Thayer, October 6, 1966. LAURENCE J. SULLIVAN SPC5, 111-CC-36648, NARA.

Anti-war protest at the Pentagon in Washington, D.C., October 22, 1967. MARTIN KONDRECK, SFC, 111-CC-46381, NATIONAL ARCHIVES AND RECORDS ADMINISTRATION, COLLEGE PARK, MD.

the War in Vietnam, it organized an October demonstration in Washington and was involved in similar protests throughout the United States. These protest organizations were encouraged by a growing opposition to the war within Congress. While only two U.S. senators, Wayne Morse (D-Oregon) and Ernest Gruening (D-Alaska), had opposed the Gulf of Tonkin Resolution in August

1964, more senators and representatives from both parties began to voice concern and opposition to the war. Some of these individuals would play a significant role in the national election in 1968.

Early Air War (1961–1968)

Concurrent with the ground war in Vietnam, the United States conducted a complex and sophisticated

Anti-war protesters are restrained at the entrance to the Pentagon in Washington, D.C., October 21, 1967. MORRIS MCMILLAN, SFC, 111-CC-46355, NATIONAL ARCHIVES AND RECORDS ADMINISTRATION, COLLEGE PARK, MD.

North Vietnam

Rolling
Thunder

Laos

BARREL ROLL

DMZ

STEEL
TIGER

TIGER
HOUND

**South
Vietnam**

Cambodia

Air campaigns map

air war in Southeast Asia, involv-
ing operations in North and South
Vietnam and Laos before 1968.
Americans were involved in air
campaigns as early as 1954, when
US personnel supported the French
defense of Dien Bien Phu, though

American pilots were not committed to the fighting. After the
end of the First Indochina War, US
Air Force advisers used American
aircraft to train South Vietnam's
air force. In the early 1960s, the
United States also committed

M-48 tank, 1966. J. HALLAS, CPL, 127-N-A186810, NARA.

aircraft to reconnaissance missions over Laos and Vietnam as well as defoliation operations under Operation Ranch Hand. In addition to Operation Pierce Arrow in 1964 after the Gulf of Tonkin incident, the United States initiated Operation Barrel Roll in northern Laos in December 1964 to support the Laotians in their conflict with the North Vietnamese Army and the Laotian Communist insurgency, the Pathet Lao.

After Operation Flaming Dart, and with the introduction of Operation Rolling Thunder in 1965, US air operations intensified. Rolling Thunder missions were designed to punish the North Vietnamese for their activities in the South. They were also used to try to convince the North Vietnamese to negotiate a peaceful settlement to the war. Both objectives proved elusive during the operation. As the war intensified and more Americans were inserted into combat roles, Rolling Thunder goals expanded. The United States used the air missions to interdict North Vietnamese personnel and supplies from entering the South in support of the attrition strategy as well as to inflict significant damage on the North's military infrastructure. In some respects, the operation was successful, as strategic assets

in the North were destroyed or severely damaged and Hanoi had to devote increased resources to move the necessary personnel and supplies down the Ho Chi Minh Trail to support its forces and allies in the South. However, the limited and restrictive nature of the air sorties (one air sortie equaled one aircraft flown in one mission) hampered its effectiveness before the operation ended in November 1968.

Working in conjunction with Rolling Thunder, the United States also initiated an air interdiction campaign in southern Laos known as Operation Steel Tiger. These air missions continued through 1968, though a portion of the area of responsibility was reassigned to MACV in December 1965 in order to better coordinate military and air operations. The new operation, Tiger Hound, retained the same objectives. All of the interdiction missions over Laos were eventually consolidated in Operation Commando Hunt in 1968. While the air campaigns over North Vietnam and Laos are generally the ones connected with the American war in Vietnam, air operations over South Vietnam accounted for most of the sorties flown during the war. The United States employed both fixed-wing aircraft and helicopters for a variety of missions, including

ground support, close air support, search-and-rescue, transportation, and other actions designed to supplement these efforts. One such mission was Arc Light sorties.

These missions involved the B-52 bomber, which struck at predetermined targets based on available intelligence. The Arc Light missions began on June 18, 1965, and were flown over South Vietnam and Laos. Because of the potential devastation the bombers could inflict within a concentrated area, the missions were highly restrictive and, in the case of Laos, required the approval of the American ambassador before they could proceed. These missions continued through 1973, when the last American combat personnel left Vietnam.

Another key aspect of the air war was air mobility, generally in the form of the helicopter, which became an iconic symbol of the American war in Vietnam. The helicopter allowed for the rapid transportation of troops into and out of areas that might otherwise have been inaccessible, and it provided reinforcement, relief, and evacuation of troops engaged with the enemy. Several models of the UH-1 Iroquois, known as the Huey, saw service in Southeast Asia. This helicopter, along with the AH-1 Huey Cobra, is the most recognizable of the war.

◄ Operation Macon, 1966. 127-N-A187574, NARA.

F-4 Phantoms, 1969. PHOTOGRAPH COURTESY OF JACK YUSKA.

B-52 Stratofortress. SERGEANT RICHARD J. MAZAUSKAS, 342-AF-109171AF, NATIONAL ARCHIVES AND RECORDS ADMINISTRATION, COLLEGE PARK, MD.

As both the air and the ground war progressed, however, it became clear to the United States that there could be no lasting victory in South Vietnam unless the people were both protected and able to protect themselves.

Winning the Hearts and Minds

The objective of winning the hearts and minds of the Vietnamese people by protecting them from the Viet Cong and North Vietnamese armies and improving their day-to-day conditions had its roots in the late 1950s. The first attempt coincided with the formation of the Republic of Vietnam as it dealt with the influx of more than eight hundred thousand refugees from the North after the 1954 Geneva Agreements. The challenge overwhelmed the Saigon government, which soon requested American assistance to provide relief and resettlement support to the refugees. When the Communist insurgency intensified its efforts to destabilize the rule of Ngo Dinh Diem in the late 1950s, the Saigon government turned to pacification efforts to separate the people from the insurgents. In July 1959, Ngo Dinh Diem announced the formation of the Agroville Program with the objective of concentrating large rural populations for mutual protection. Agrovilles would also offer inhabitants all of the amenities they lacked in the countryside, such as electricity, schools, and medical facilities. The program, however, failed to achieve its objectives due to its faulty implementation and the inability of the Saigon government to provide the necessary support to the agrovilles. Additionally, the Vietnamese people who participated in the program were often forcibly removed from their homes and inserted into living conditions that failed to live up to the promise. The insurgency was also able to penetrate the agrovilles, which negated one of their primary values. Unable to either protect the people or offer improvements, the program ended in 1961 and was soon replaced with another effort.

The Strategic Hamlet Program originated in 1962. It had similar objectives to the Agroville Program, though its implementation was designed to avoid the failures of its predecessor. Under the leadership of Ngo Dinh Nhu, the Strategic Hamlet Program tried to limit the need to relocate people from their villages by designing defenses around existing hamlets. The result was several thousand more strategic hamlets planned than agrovilles. The program originated with the Vietnamese, but its ownership and direction were soon contested by the

UH-1B helicopter delivering water to an outpost in Tay Ninh Province. VIETNAM PHOTO SERVICE, 64-5381, NATIONAL ARCHIVES AND RECORDS ADMINISTRATION, COLLEGE PARK, MD.

UH-1D helicopters airlifting members of the 2nd Battalion, 14th Infantry Regiment during Operation Wahiawa, May 16, 1966. JAMES K. F. DUNG, SFC, 111-CC-34613, NATIONAL ARCHIVES AND RECORDS ADMINISTRATION, COLLEGE PARK, MD.

United States, which was less willing to allow another failed attempt by the Saigon government to go forward. American support for Ngo Dinh Diem was waning. The United States called in Sir Robert Thompson to help guide the program. Thompson, a British counterinsurgency expert who had some success against a Communist insurgency in Malaya in the 1950s, incorporated some of the Vietnamese concepts for the program, but he disagreed with Ngo Dinh Nhu on the best way to deal with the development of the strategic hamlets. Ngo Dinh Nhu advocated a holistic approach, which meant building as many strategic hamlets as possible at the same time, whereas Thompson wanted to employ a more methodical tactic that established one strong strategic hamlet in a contested area before additional ones were built. Because the program existed during a time of both political and military upheaval in Vietnam, it did not survive. The program ended in 1964, and pacification of the countryside was suspended as the Americanization of the war commenced.

Another American strategy was employed as the Strategic Hamlet Program ended. Originating from the Central Intelligence Agency, the creation of the People's Action Teams sought to insert armed personnel into the villages to counter the influence of the Viet Cong. This program evolved into the Revolutionary Development Cadres by February 1966. This new group organized fifty-nine-man mobile groups that traveled between hamlets to assist in the day-to-day needs of the people as well as help improve the infrastructure of the hamlets. The Revolutionary Development Cadres program was not well organized and had to compete for limited US resources with other military and civil efforts engaged in pacification.

Firmly entrenched in Vietnam by 1967, the United States began to recognize the importance of pacification as part of its overall strategy for victory. Earlier, in November 1966, it created the Office of Civil Operations to administer civilian pacification efforts. Both military and civilian programs were then organized under the Civil Operations and Revolutionary Development Support (CORDS) on May 10, 1967. Under the direction of Robert Komer, who answered only to General Westmoreland in Vietnam, CORDS made major advances in pacification with such programs as Chieu Hoi, which rallied North Vietnamese and Viet Cong defectors. It also created New Life Villages, which applied the earlier benefits of the Strategic Hamlet Program, as well as the

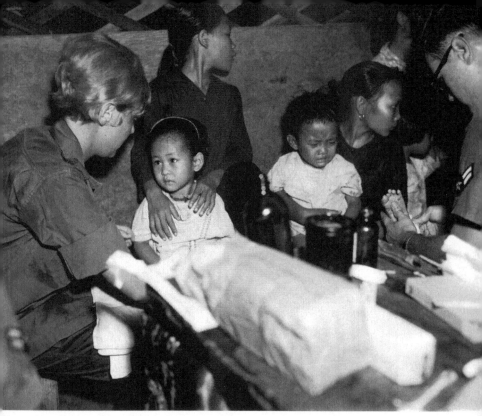

Civic action team provides medical treatment to Vietnamese in the countryside, 1967.
342-KKE-28429, NATIONAL ARCHIVES AND RECORDS ADMINISTRATION, COLLEGE PARK, MD.

Phoenix Program, which targeted the infrastructure of the Viet Cong. Pacification was severely disrupted with the 1968 Tet Offensive, as all efforts were redirected toward defending or recouping the gains made during the nationwide offensive against South Vietnam.

Naval Operations

In conjunction with Operation Rolling Thunder and the insertion of combat troops into South Vietnam, the United States Navy also made its presence felt in Southeast Asia. On March 11, it initiated Operation Market Time, a naval interdiction program designed to stop the flow of personnel and supplies traveling by water across the Demilitarized Zone. The navy created Task Force 115 (Coastal Surveillance Force) on July 31, which established three layers of defense from the coastline to approximately 150 miles out to sea from the Gulf of Tonkin to the Gulf of Thailand. The action proved to be very successful and forced the North Vietnamese and Viet Cong to switch their focus to the Ho Chi Minh Trail through Laos and Cambodia, using the neutral Cambodian port of Sihanoukville to supply their forces.

The navy recognized that a truly effective interdiction campaign required the control of all of the inland waterways in South Vietnam. This proved to be a difficult challenge, as there were more than three thousand nautical miles of waterways that the enemy could use to transport its personnel and supplies. On December 18, the navy created Task Force 116 (River Patrol Force) under Operation Game Warden to monitor the waterways and interdict suspicious craft. In 1966, Task Force 117 (Mobile Riverine Force) was included in the US arsenal. It used a combination of air, ground, and sea assets to coordinate a more efficient interdiction program, and it took the fight to areas that the enemy had considered safe. The Mobile Riverine Force operated pri-

MEDCAP visit to the village of Phu Gia near Phu Cat Air Base, January 23, 1970.
JOE MALBROUGH, A1C, 342-AF-106667AF, NATIONAL ARCHIVES AND RECORDS ADMINISTRATION, COLLEGE PARK, MD.

Operation Farafot IV in Phan Rang, March 1967. PFC DARRYL ARIZO, 111-SC-639445, NARA.

marily in the Mekong Delta region to the south of Saigon. It was not until after the 1968 Tet Offensive that the three separate task forces were united in their efforts.

On October 18, 1968, Vice Admiral Elmo R. Zumwalt Jr., who commanded Naval Forces, Vietnam, created the Southeast Asia Lake Ocean River Delta Strategy (SEALORDS). SEALORDS reorganized the American Naval assets in South Vietnam into one force, though it adapted all of the objectives of the earlier task forces. Zumwalt believed in using the waterways of South Vietnam to the United States' benefit and taking the battle to the North Vietnamese and Viet Cong. He also authorized a series of operations designed to use the existing canal and river network on the western side of South Vietnam to create a barrier from the Gulf of Thailand to a position northwest of Saigon. The 250-mile barrier became an effective way of limiting the enemy's influence in the Mekong Delta. SEALORDS

United States naval advisers to the South Vietnam Coastal Junk Force keep watch while South Vietnamese Junk Force personnel inspect a boat stopped in South Vietnamese waters. UNITED STATES NAVY #1111611, 66-3818, NATIONAL ARCHIVES AND RECORDS ADMINISTRATION, COLLEGE PARK, MD.

ended in April 1971 as part of the Nixon administration's strategy to end the American war.

A Light at the End of the Tunnel

American military operations in Southeast Asia continued to inflict serious damage on both North Vietnamese and Viet Cong forces. However, the strategy of attrition did not seem to be taking hold, and the enemy appeared to be strong despite its continued heavy losses. Major operations such as Cedar Falls and Junction City sought to eliminate the Viet Cong threat from strategic areas to the north of Saigon. In January 1967, Cedar Falls involved more than thirty thousand allied troops but failed to dislodge the Viet Cong from the Thanh Dien Forest Reserve, which was the home of its headquarters for the region. The February–May 1967 Operation Junction City struck at the area known as the Iron Triangle, or War Zone C, a strategic location to the northwest of Saigon. In both operations, as in so many in the war to date, the Viet Cong were able to avoid a major engagement and remained an influential presence in the contested areas.

In late fall 1967, the Johnson administration hoped to rally the American people and the international community by orchestrating a public relations campaign. Those within the Johnson administration and MACV believed the timing to be right, as it appeared the United States had finally gained the upper hand in the war. Westmoreland was recalled to Washington to participate in this campaign and was joined by Johnson, Secretary of State Dean Rusk, and members of the Joint Chiefs of Staff, who all argued that the enemy had been dealt a severe blow and that the United States now held the initiative. By the end of January 1968, these confident statements were put to the test when the North Vietnamese and Viet Cong launched a nationwide offensive in South Vietnam.

1968 Tet Offensive

The Tet Offensive began on January 31. The objective of the attack was to cause as much damage to American and South Vietnamese forces as possible and set the stage for a national uprising of the people against the Saigon government. The offensive was preceded by an attack against the marine base at Khe

◀ Patrolling the Cai Ngay Canal, April 1970. PHC HILL, 428-K-83565, NATIONAL ARCHIVES AND RECORDS ADMINISTRATION, COLLEGE PARK, MD.

Sanh, which was situated near the Demilitarized Zone. The North Vietnamese hoped that the United States would focus on Khe Sanh, which would allow for an element of surprise. After the offensive began, the United States would then have to make the choice of concentrating its efforts on either Khe Sanh or the major urban population centers under attack. The North Vietnamese hoped that the battle for Khe Sanh would duplicate the success it had had at Dien Bien Phu in 1954 and, at the same time, relieve pressure on the Ho Chi Minh Trail, which had suffered as a result of American interdiction activities.

The North Vietnamese and Viet Cong massed approximately twenty thousand personnel around the six thousand marines defending at Khe Sanh. Initial attacks against the base in the weeks preceding the Tet Offensive failed to make any gains. As Tet approached, the North Vietnamese turned to artillery and mortar barrages to keep the marines occupied and the American military focused on Khe Sanh. This allowed thousands of troops to infiltrate the major cities and establish forward positions throughout the country in anticipation of the main attack. When Tet arrived on January 31, the offensive commenced. The

North Vietnamese and Viet Cong attacked in every province in Vietnam, but their main efforts were against Saigon and Hue.

In Saigon, the attackers hit such strategic targets as the US embassy, MACV compound, Saigon Radio facility, presidential palace, and Tan Son Nhut airfield, though with little headway. Despite the defeat of the initial assault, fighting continued in Saigon, with intense action in the Cho Lon suburb that lasted through February. The North Vietnamese and Viet Cong forces were routed, but they inflicted significant damage on the city and worsened the plight of the already war-weary population.

In the ancient imperial capital of Hue, the citadel was the main target, though there were other strategic sites, such as the University of Hue. Most of the citadel was occupied, and it was not recaptured until the end of February. Like Saigon, the fighting in Hue created a refugee crisis as homes and businesses were destroyed in the fighting. Upon recapturing the citadel, the South Vietnamese and Americans found mass grave sites that contained the bodies of more than three thousand Vietnamese who had been executed because of their support for the Saigon government.

◄ Soldiers from the 25th Infantry Division, August 31, 1967. PAUL D. HALVERSON, SPC4, 111-SC-642158, NARA.

Vietnamese victims of the Hue Massacre, 1968. SOURCE JUSPAO, 71-443, NATIONAL ARCHIVES AND RECORDS ADMINISTRATION, COLLEGE PARK, MD.

The Tet Offensive failed to accomplish its main objectives. The North Vietnamese and Viet Cong attack did not result in the uprising of the people, nor were the fighting capabilities of the United States or South Vietnamese significantly diminished. The attack instead exposed the Viet Cong, who suf-fered disproportionate casualties and became ineffective until their numbers could be replaced. Khe Sanh held, and the South Vietnam-ese forces found themselves equal to the task of defending against a large-scale, organized attack. However, even though the offensive was a military success for the United

AMERICANIZATION OF THE VIETNAM WAR

States and South Vietnam, there was political and psychological backlash to it. The Johnson administration's public relations campaign indicating that the war was nearly over was in shambles. It was difficult to reconcile how an enemy on the verge of defeat could launch such a massive and coordinated offensive. Johnson went on the defensive as his Vietnam policy was questioned by a growing number of people who were not traditionally part of the anti-war movement, including members of his own party who had previously supported the administration's strategy in Southeast Asia. As a result, Johnson would make a series of decisions that altered the scene both in the United States and in Vietnam.

After Tet

The Tet Offensive was a military victory for the United States and South Vietnam, though it caused both a political and a psychological setback. For the South Vietnamese, the number of refugees created by the urban fighting stretched an already fragile domestic infrastructure. The ARVN had proven its worth, but it also suffered casualties that needed to be replaced. For those in the United States opposed to the war, the Tet Offensive reaffirmed that the end of the war was not in sight, contrary to Westmoreland's claims that the enemy had been defeated on the battlefield. Within the Democratic Party, Johnson faced a serious leadership challenge when Senator Eugene McCarthy (D-Minnesota) received a surprising number of votes in the New Hampshire primary. This first primary in the process of determining the Democratic nominee for the 1968 presidential election came as a shock to many in the White House who believed that the incumbent would not face such early opposition. That McCarthy ran on an anti-war platform was not encouraging. Four days after the March 12 primary, McCarthy's success encouraged Senator Robert Kennedy (D-New York) to announce his candidacy for the nomination. With the nomination process less certain after these two events, Johnson made the situation even more complicated when he declared in a national televised speech on March 31 that he would neither seek nor accept his party's nomination for the presidency.

This decision, coupled with another announcement in the same speech that the United States would scale down Operation Rolling Thunder and focus on the area to the north of the Demilitarized Zone, brought varied and intense reaction. While there were some who sympathized with the

president and his justification for the announcement, many within the anti-war movement saw the speech as an admission of fault for the United States' involvement in Southeast Asia. Others sought to take advantage of the political opportunities available now that Johnson was out of the election, while a general sense of malaise, and in some cases betrayal, permeated the US military force.

Regardless of the reaction, it seemed inevitable that the Democratic nominating convention, which was to be held in Chicago that summer, would be contested. With Johnson out of the race, the party turned to Vice President Hubert Humphrey as its choice. When Robert Kennedy was assassinated in June after winning the California primary and McCarthy's momentum was checked earlier by Kennedy's addition to the process, it seemed that Humphrey would earn the nomination without controversy. However, those who had supported the anti-war candidates, and many who were also reeling from the earlier assassination of civil rights leader Martin Luther King Jr., seemed intent on making the convention a nexus for those opposed to the war and the civil injustice they perceived pervading American society.

The August 1968 Democratic Nominating Convention was the site of intense protest against the Vietnam War and included a younger group of individuals dedicated to social justice. Delegates who had been supporters of the anti-war candidates within the convention disrupted proceedings in clashes with those who wanted Humphrey to succeed Johnson. Outside the convention in the streets, the demonstrations turned violent as Chicago's mayor, Richard Daley, authorized the city's police to use whatever means necessary to break up the protesting groups. The result, filmed and broadcast around the country, was a scene of violence and mayhem that called into question the very democratic process that was being undertaken within the convention hall. Humphrey won the nomination, much to the chagrin of the anti-war delegates who made up a majority of those voting. In contrast, the Republican Nominating Convention, held earlier in the month in Miami, was the mirror opposite of the chaos in Chicago. Richard Nixon won on

◄ Cholon after the Tet Offensive, February 1968. T.L. LAWSON, PH1, 428-N-1130131, NATIONAL ARCHIVES AND RECORDS ADMINISTRATION, COLLEGE PARK, MD.

William C. Westmoreland (1914–2005)

January–June 1964	Deputy Commander, MACV
June 1964–June 1968	Commander, MACV
July 1968–June 1972	Chief of Staff of the United States Army

Secretary of Defense Robert S. McNamara (left) and General William C. Westmoreland (right) visit American troops in Danang, August 1965.
J.F. FRALEY, 127-N-A184852, NATIONAL ARCHIVES AND RECORDS ADMINISTRATION, COLLEGE PARK, MD.

President Lyndon B. Johnson and General William C. Westmoreland discussing
◀ Vietnam in the post-Tet period, April 1968. WHITE HOUSE, 68-1303, NATIONAL ARCHIVES AND RECORDS ADMINISTRATION, COLLEGE PARK, MD.

AMERICANIZATION OF THE VIETNAM WAR

Marines aboard an M-48 tank southwest of Phu Bai, April 3, 1968. D.I. FISHER, CPL, 127-N-A371493, NARA.

the first ballot and would go on to win the 1968 presidential election.

Westmoreland became another victim of the Tet Offensive, though he had indicated that his plans to leave the position of MACV commander had been in place before it. Immediately after the offensive began, Westmoreland requested 206,000 additional troops to reinforce defensive positions but also to go on the offensive in the countryside where the Viet Cong infrastructure had been severely damaged. On the heels of both public and media criticism for the failure to anticipate the Tet attacks and backlash over the public relations

campaign in the months preceding the offensive, Johnson refused the request. Eventually, about a quarter of the number of troops requested made their way to Vietnam and easily handled two smaller offensives later in the year. In July, General Creighton Abrams took over from Westmoreland.

Westmoreland's request for reinforcements at the outset of the offensive was also geared toward a new plan for pacification. The Tet Offensive had disrupted pacification efforts, but after the defeat of the Viet Cong, who had left the anonymity and safety of the countryside to strike at American and South Vietnamese forces, a new opportunity arose. Dubbed the Accelerated Pacification Campaign, Robert Komer wanted to fill the vacuum in the countryside, which was created by Viet Cong losses. He was frustrated, however, by President Nguyen Van Thieu, who did not want to release ARVN forces protecting the urban centers and military facilities. Nguyen Van Thieu believed another offensive, as strong as the first, was coming, and he did not want to disperse his best troops into the countryside. In November, William Colby, who had replaced Komer as the head of CORDS, was able to convince the Vietnamese to act. While several months had been lost to indecision, the new pacification efforts did challenge the North Vietnamese and Viet Cong in the countryside. Such organizations as the Regional Forces and Popular Forces received modern weapons and checked enemy operations while the People's Self-Defense Force offered a military presence in nearly every village. These efforts would again be disrupted in 1972 when the North Vietnamese launched their Easter Offensive.

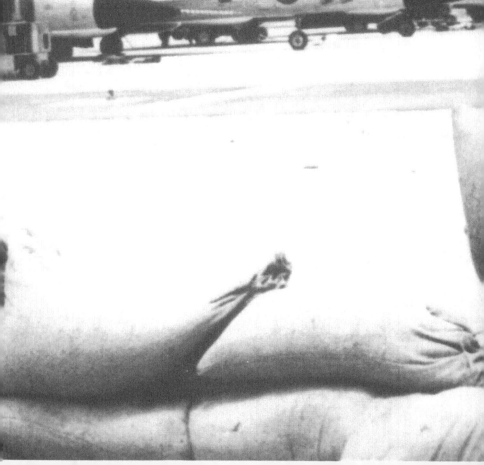

CHAPTER 7

NIXON'S VIETNAM

The animosity between Cambodia and South Vietnam predates the First Indochina War, as it was the Vietnamese who conquered territory from the Khmer Kingdom of Angkor to establish the southern end of their country. Like Vietnam, Cambodia was a part of French Indochina but received its independence in 1953. After the 1954 Geneva Conference, Cambodia declared its neutrality, though it had numerous border incidents with South Vietnam through the 1950s. Cambodia's ruler, Norodom Sihanouk, refused to declare support for either of the two Vietnams, but in the 1950s it became clear that he was more sympathetic to the North than the South. Ngo Dinh Diem continually warned the United States that Cambodia harbored Vietnamese insurgents and allowed the North Vietnamese free transit through the eastern end of its country but was never able to persuade the Americans to act against this clear violation of Cambodia's neutral stance.

When the United States introduced combat troops into South

Operation around My Tho, April 5, 1968. DENNIS KURPUIS, SPEC. 4, 111-CC-47777, NARA.

Vietnam and began its naval operations to interdict the flow of North Vietnamese supplies moving into South Vietnam by sea, Cambodia's importance increased. The North Vietnamese accelerated their development of the Ho Chi Minh Trail, which crossed the southeast portion of Laos and the northeastern section of Cambodia. It also made arrangements for neutral ships to enter the port of Sihanoukville and offload supplies for its forces along the Cambodian–South Vietnamese border. In return, the Vietnamese promised to contain their forces along the border and offered a portion of the supplies to the Cambodians. As the war intensified in the mid-1960s, Sihanouk continued to maintain Cambodia's neutrality. However, he failed to live up to that policy. The Johnson administration chose not to confront Cambodia on its duplicity, instead trying a diplomatic route to dissuade the Cambodians from their alleged neutralist position. US forces were prohibited from crossing the border into Cambodia as it conducted its war in South Vietnam. The ability of the North Vietnamese and Viet Cong to use Cambodia as a safe haven when under pursuit or as a staging area for operations into South Vietnam caused significant criticism among US military leaders, who believed such restrictions gave the enemy an advantage and allowed them to persist. By 1969, it is estimated that nearly forty thousand soldiers were using bases in Cambodia to conduct operations against South Vietnam.

The Johnson administration chose not to confront Cambodia. The same would not be true when Richard Nixon entered the White House. Concurrent with a new US policy for how the war would be conducted, the North Vietnamese and Viet Cong also changed tactics as a result of their defeat during the Tet Offensive. They began to levy taxes from Cambodians within their control and conscripted individuals to build roads and installations. These Cambodians replaced the Vietnamese lost in the offensive. North Vietnam also engaged in a scheme to pay a higher-than-market value for rice, the primary staple of the Cambodian diet, which destabilized its economy. These aggressive moves coupled with activities designed to support the Communist insurgency movement in Cambodia,

led by the Khmer Rouge, made the Cambodians more amenable to American requests to acknowledge and help eliminate the Vietnamese presence in their country.

The Nixon administration adapted to these changing conditions by ordering a secret bombing campaign against Vietnamese-held territory in Cambodia. On March 18, 1969, Operation Menu sent air sorties against known North Vietnamese and Viet Cong positions along the Cambodia–South Vietnam border in order to disrupt any offensive actions. The operation proved successful but was eventually exposed by the *New York Times* on May 2, 1970, after another operation in Cambodian territory commenced. The US incursion into Cambodia resulted from a series of events that occurred in that country and supplemented the Nixon administration policy for ending the war.

In 1968, the then presidential candidate for the Republican Party, Richard Nixon, campaigned on a platform of initiating a plan to decrease the costly war in Vietnam by handing over the main fighting responsibilities to South Vietnam. After winning the presidential election, Nixon implemented this policy, which became known as Vietnamization. The plan was formalized on July 25, 1969, during a press conference in Guam, during which time Nixon announced plans to increase ARVN training with improved equipment. Nixon had already authorized the withdrawal of 25,000 soldiers without replacement the previous month and would agree to the removal of an additional 150,000 by the end of 1969. Vietnamization promised an end to the American war in Vietnam, but it required some actions that inflamed the anti-war movement, which was cautious of the president.

For Vietnamization to succeed, the United States needed to give the ARVN forces time to train and take over the responsibilities held by the American military. This process took much longer than many who were opposed to the war believed necessary. It also meant that the North Vietnamese and Viet Cong threat needed to be diminished. The secret bombings and 1970

President-elect Richard M. Nixon with President Lyndon B. Johnson, December 12, 1968. STAFF-PINTO, 68-4004, NATIONAL ARCHIVES AND RECORDS ADMINISTRATION, COLLEGE PARK, MD.

Captured weapons, 1968. PHOTOGRAPH COURTESY OF JACK YUSKA.

Cambodian incursion were directly related to this requirement. The Nixon administration believed these short periods of escalation would accelerate Vietnamization. However, Vietnamization also had a negative impact on some of the American soldiers fighting in Vietnam. While there was a general feeling of relief that the war would end soon, not many cherished the idea of being the last soldier killed. Vietnamization succeeded as a plan for the United States to disengage from Southeast Asia, but it failed to ensure the survival of its longtime ally, the Republic of Vietnam.

In August 1969, in response to domestic anti-Communist pressure, Sihanouk formed a new government with Lon Nol as the prime minister and Prince Sisowath Sirik Matak as deputy prime minister. Both men opposed the Vietnamese military personnel in their country and clashed with Sihanouk on Cambodian foreign policy. When Sihanouk traveled to France in January 1970, the two men conspired against him and, on March 18, 1970, encouraged the Cambodian national assembly to meet secretly to vote Sihanouk out of power.

The bloodless coup d'état pushed Sihanouk further into the Communist sphere and an alliance with the Communist coalition group, the Indochinese People's United Front.

Exiled in China, Sihanouk created a Royal Government of National Union, which he claimed was the real Cambodian government, and publicly supported the Khmer Rouge. The political instability caused by these events allowed the North Vietnamese and Viet Cong to increase their pressure westward toward the capital of Phnom Penh. When that city was threatened, Lon Nol appealed for international assistance. The Nixon administration, which had been closely following the situation and was already committed to a secret bombing campaign, agreed to support the Cambodian military and orchestrated an incursion from South Vietnam across the Cambodian border to destroy the Vietnamese personnel and facilities established there.

The United States limited its incursion into Cambodia to sixty days, though the ARVN forces involved remained for ninety days. The results of the military operation, which began on May 1, were mixed. While the combined forces were not able to draw the enemy into a major battle, they did inflict some casualties on the forces stationed in Cambodia and destroyed significant supplies that had been stockpiled for future operations. However, the incursion aided the Khmer Rouge, who, with active North Vietnamese aid, established a stronghold in the northeastern part of the country. This allowed the Khmer Rouge to slowly gain territory and influence in Cambodia. The military operation also resulted in a resurgence of the anti-war movement, which saw the incursion as an expansion of the war rather than a means to decrease the time the United States needed to hand over responsibilities for conducting operations to the ARVN through Vietnamization.

The anti-war movement responded to the Cambodian incursion with a series of demonstrations that affected all levels of American society. It also led to confrontations between protesters and members of the National Guard and local police forces. At Kent State University, demonstrations against the incursion started on May 1 and quickly escalated as the ROTC building on campus was razed to the ground and National Guard personnel arrived to restore order. On May 4, the two groups clashed, resulting in the death of four students and the wounding of nine others. The severity of the incident shocked the nation, as did another clash at Jackson State University on May 14 when two students were killed in an altercation between protesters and the police. These two events were among many across university and college campuses,

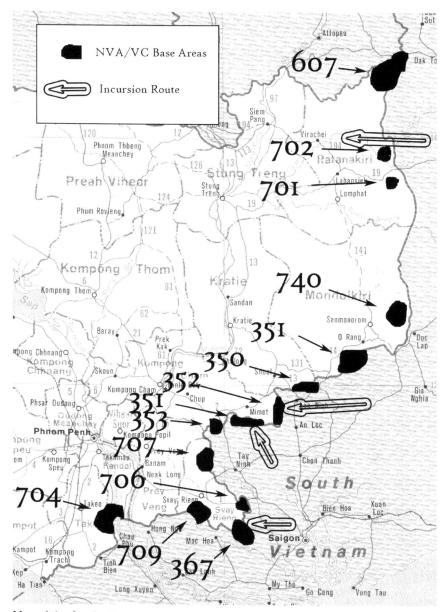

Map of the Cambodian incursion

RONALD B. FRANKUM JR., *Like Rolling Thunder: The Air War in Vietnam, 1964–1975*
(LANHAM, MD: ROWMAN & LITTLEFIELD, 2005), 138.

EFT
VIET-NAM
MARCH
APRIL
MAY
JUNE
JULY
AUGUST
SEPTEMBER
NOVEMBER
DECEMBER
JANUARY
FEBUARY
515
HOME

some of which were shut down, as demonstrations made it difficult to continue daily operations.

Congressional opposition to the war in Southeast Asia also intensified. Earlier, Senators John Sherman Cooper (R-Kentucky) and Frank Church (D-Idaho) added an amendment to the Foreign Military Sales Act that prohibited US combat troops in Cambodia after July 1, 1970, and congressional approval for any additional US activities in Southeast Asia. Nixon threatened to veto the act if it included the Cooper-Church amendment, and the House of Representatives rejected the amendment. Cooper and Church offered a revised version of the amendment to the Supplementary Foreign Assistance Act of 1970, which passed in both the House of Representatives and the Senate on December 22, 1970. Because the incursion had already ended, this newer version was less restrictive, but it did signal a shift in the balance of power between the executive branch and Congress in matters of foreign relations.

Laos

The success of the Cambodian incursion in disrupting the enemy's plans for further offensives into South Vietnam emboldened the Nixon administration to shift its focus to neighboring Laos. The country's southeastern section had been a conduit for North Vietnamese personnel and supplies into South Vietnam ever since the closing of the sea routes with Operation Market Time. Laos bordered North Vietnam to the east and Cambodia and South Vietnam to the south and southeast. Its strategic value due to its proximity was not lost on any of the belligerents. As one of the three countries that made up French Indochina, Laos was relatively unaffected by the First Indochina War. It was influenced by the Communist movement in North Vietnam, however. Under the leadership of Prince Souphanouvong, the Pathet Lao organization worked against French colonialism, and after the 1954 Geneva Agreements its political party, the Neo Lao Hak Xat, vied for power with the Laotian Royal Government. Laos underwent political instability in the late 1950s and early 1960s and was, at one point, the focus of US efforts in Southeast Asia. In 1961, the United States helped to organize a conference at Geneva, Switzerland, to solve the Laotian situation. The 1962 Geneva Accords on Laos offered neutrality to that country,

◄ Soldier from the 1st Cavalry Division during Operation Pershing, 1968.
FRANK MOFFITT, SPCS, 111-SC-647323, NARA.

NIXON'S VIETNAM

but the North Vietnamese violated that position before the year was out. The South Vietnamese opposed the conference and its agreements. Ngo Dinh Diem did not trust the Pathet Lao or North Vietnamese to respect the agreements. He asserted that neutrality was not a viable option in Southeast Asia.

The Royal Laotian Army fought a long but low-intensity war against the Pathet Lao and its allies. The area of fighting was in the Plain of Jars and was dictated by both the diverse topography and the country's climate. During the dry season, the North Vietnamese and Pathet Lao conducted offensive operations against the outnumbered Royal Laotian Army. The United States provided air-to-ground support, under Operation Barrel Roll, in an

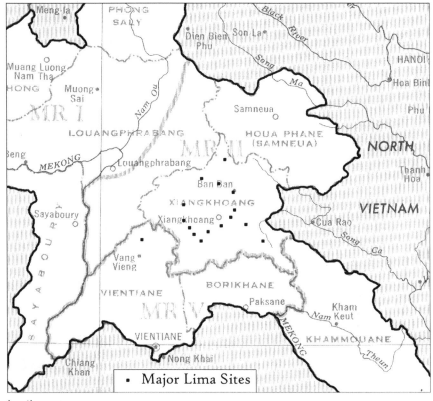

Laotian map

RONALD B. FRANKUM JR., *Like Rolling Thunder: The Air war in Vietnam, 1964–1975* (LANHAM, MD: ROWMAN & LITTLEFIELD, 2005), 125.

NIXON'S VIETNAM

Soldiers from the 101st Airborne Division near Tam Ky, June 2, 1969.
STEPHEN KLUBOCK, SPCS, 111-SC-650496, NARA.

attempt to hold ground in the Plain of Jars. The two sides shifted the initiative in the monsoon season as the United States focused its air power on air mobility to concentrate Laotian forces against weaker Pathet Lao positions in order to regain lost territory. Throughout the Plain of Jars, tall rock outcroppings known as Lima Sites dominated the battlefield and became the focal points for intense fighting. The two sides conducted this type of back-and-forth warfare until 1973.

Unlike South Vietnam, the United States did not send combat troops to Laos. Instead, it concentrated its support for the Laotians with air power. Operation Barrel Roll in the North and Steel Tiger and Tiger Hound in the South were the results. However, because of Laotian neutrality, the war was conducted under conditions that were as secret as possible. The political conditions in the United States prohibited the introduction of combat forces, just as they did in Cambodia. When

Soldier from the 5th Infantry Division during Operation Utah Mesa in the A Shau Valley, July 1969. RONALD HAMMEREN, SPCS, 111-SC-651203, NARA.

Nixon entered the White House—and on the heels of the Cambodian incursion—the situation changed.

In order to allow Vietnamization more time to progress, the Nixon administration encouraged a 1971 ARVN ground operation in Laos to sever the Ho Chi Minh Trail. With the North Vietnamese in Cambodia in disarray, a successful Laotian operation would significantly hinder the ability of the North Vietnamese to maintain their forces in South Vietnam. However, the December 1970 Cooper-Church amendment prohibited the United States from joining the South Vietnamese operation. Instead, the United States provided air assets. Operation Lam Son 719 had as its objective the city of Tchepone and the destruction of North Vietnamese and Viet Cong personnel and supplies stockpiled near it. Unlike the Cambodian incursion, Lam Son 719 was not an efficient military action. Miscommunication and poor leadership mired the ARVN force while Nguyen Van Thieu interfered with the operation, which caused a near military disaster. Because of the heightened strategic importance of Tchepone and the Ho Chi Ming Trail after Cambodia, the North Vietnamese and Viet Cong chose to fight rather than retreat further into the interior of Laos. As a result, South Vietnamese forces were nearly surrounded and faced a combination of heavy artillery and tanks that threatened to eliminate the entire task force.

Despite the precarious position of the ARVN units, Nguyen Van Thieu authorized his forces to seize Tchepone, which they did, although the city had been vacated by the enemy. Proclaiming victory, he then ordered his troops to return. This proved impossible, as the North Vietnamese had completed their encirclement of the ARVN force that had gone too far into Laos. The ARVN lost nearly 50 percent of its personnel to casualties, while the United States suffered significant damage to its helicopters that had been sent in to save the situation. After the end of Lam Son 719, both Nixon and Nguyen Van Thieu declared that the operation had been successful. There were few others who agreed. For many congressional opponents to Nixon's Vietnam War strategy, the use of Americans in the operation violated the spirit, if not the law, of the Cooper-Church amendment. Future congressional action to limit the ability of the executive to wage war and diplomacy would make sure that their directives were clear.

Map of Lam Son 719

1972 Easter Offensive

The failure of Operation Lam Son 719, coupled with Vietnamization and the 1972 presidential election in the United States, encouraged the North Vietnamese to take a calculated risk in launching an invasion of South Vietnam. The Easter Offensive was the largest attack by Communist forces since the Korean War and involved more than two hundred thousand personnel before it ended in failure. The North Vietnamese believed that the ARVN forces, given their struggles in Laos, would not be able to react to the massive attack without US ground support, which had been reduced to two combat brigades as a result of Vietnamization. They also did not think the Nixon administration would recommit to Vietnam during an election year. The objective was the destruction of the ARVN, a popular uprising, and discrediting the Nixon administration in order to give anti-war candidate George McGovern (D-South Dakota) a chance at winning the national election. In many ways, the 1972 offensive had objectives similar to those of the 1954 victory at Dien Bien Phu and the 1968 Tet Offensive. The North Vietnamese believed that the offensive would end the war. Both the United States and South Vietnam would prove the Communist assertions wrong.

The offensive was a three-pronged attack against the South. The first action occurred near the Demilitarized Zone, with the heaviest fighting occurring in Quang Tri province. The initial North Vietnamese attacks were successful, as the ARVN units were forced to abandon Quang Tri City on May 1 and were pushed back toward Hue. When North Vietnamese forces appeared to be on the brink of victory, Nguyen Van Thieu replaced I Corps commander Lieutenant General Hoang Xuan Lam with Lieutenant General Ngo Quang Truong. The reinforced ARVN forces rallied and then counterattacked. Using US air and naval gun support, the ARVN force retook Quang Tri City on September 16 and pushed the North Vietnamese back nearly to their starting point by October. Both sides suffered heavy casualties; the South also had to deal with tens of thousands of additional refugees who were now displaced because of the war.

The second attack occurred in Kontum and Pleiku provinces with the objective of securing Route 19 from the Central Highlands to the coast. A successful operation would cut the north-south Route 1 and make it difficult for the South Vietnamese to reinforce its embattled forces in Quang Tri. The attack

Map of three attacks during the Easter Offensive

RONALD B. FRANKUM JR., *Like Rolling Thunder: The Air War in Vietnam, 1964–1975*
(LANHAM, MD: ROWMAN & LITTLEFIELD, 2005), 150.

NIXON'S VIETNAM

started after the northern operation began and, similar to it, was initially successful. North Vietnamese forces placed the ARVN camps at Dak To and Tan Canh under siege and threatened Kontum by early May. As in the North, Nguyen Van Thieu replaced his commanding general; this time Major General Nguyen Van Toan entered the battlefield, and the ARVN forces were able to stabilize the front and then counterattack, with American air power, to clear the enemy out of the region. This second prong of the offensive ended by the end of June.

The third North Vietnamese thrust was in Binh Long province. The objective was the cities of Loc Ninh and An Loc, only fifteen miles from Saigon. Three Viet Cong divisions were responsible for the attack, with the goal of taking An Loc and establishing a Provisional Revolutionary Government of the Republic of South Vietnam, which would encourage the people to rise up against the Saigon government. Despite a ninety-five-day siege, the ARVN troops in An Loc held until a relief force arrived and supported a counterattack that drove the Viet Cong out of Long Binh.

The determination of the ARVN forces, supported by American firepower, ensured a costly victory for South Vietnam. The United States launched Operation Line-

President Nixon (center) with Secretary of State William Rogers (left) and National Security Adviser Dr. Henry A. Kissinger, July 18, 1971. WHITE HOUSE (6823-13), 71-3973, NATIONAL ARCHIVES AND RECORDS ADMINISTRATION, COLLEGE PARK, MD.

Dr. Henry Kissinger, January 24, 1973. UNITED STATES INFORMATION AGENCY, 73-312, NATIONAL ARCHIVES AND RECORDS ADMINISTRATION, COLLEGE PARK, MD.

backer during the attack, which dropped approximately 125,000 tons of munitions on North Vietnam. Unlike earlier air operations, the Linebacker operations were not hampered as much by restrictions, as the Nixon administration vowed to punish the overt invaders. Operation Linebacker ended on October 22, when the North Vietnamese indicated that they were willing to resume peace negotiations. The Easter Offensive had already ended or was nearing its completion in South Vietnam, and the prospects for peace seemed obtainable for the United States, as the North Vietnamese had suffered 50 percent casualties.

Peace proved elusive in the fall of 1972, as the parties involved in the negotiations failed to resolve preliminary issues that would allow for an accord to be signed. The Nixon administration became frustrated with the delays and obstinacy of the

North Vietnamese and authorized a second Linebacker operation to force the issue. Operation Linebacker II, sometimes referred to as the Christmas bombings, began on December 12 and continued, albeit with a short pause around Christmas, until December 29. The United States Air Force targeted North Vietnam's military infrastructure, delivering approximately twenty thousand tons of bombs. The North Vietnamese agreed to resume negotiations in Paris on January 8, 1973, and, on January 15, the United States suspended bombing sorties above the Demilitarized Zone. The Paris Peace Accords was signed on January 27.

Paris Peace Accords

The Agreement on Ending the War and Restoring Peace in Vietnam, more commonly known as the Paris Peace Accords, ended the Vietnam War for the United States. The document was signed by representatives from the United States, the Republic of Vietnam, the Democratic Republic of Vietnam, and the Provisional Revolutionary Government of the Republic of South Vietnam. The four protocols of the accords had a combined fifty-nine articles that covered all aspects of the peace that should have followed. However, not all of the signatories were pleased with the final document. Nguyen Van Thieu did not believe that North Vietnam would honor the peace and needed a guarantee from the Nixon administration that the United States would continue to support his country should there be any violation of the terms. While the Nixon administration provided that guarantee, it would not be able to keep this promise, as it underwent its own destruction in the Watergate scandal.

There were several articles within the Paris Peace Accords that held significant meaning for each of the belligerents. The North Vietnamese desired the withdrawal of US personnel and an end to American military activities, while the United States focused on Article 8, which called for the return of prisoners of war and the sharing of information about men who were captured or missing in action. The South Vietnamese looked to Article 9, which allowed for self-determination, and Article 15, which called for the reunification of the two Vietnams through peaceful means. The accords also covered the conflicts in Cambodia and Laos. Although the Paris Peace Accords did create an International Commission of Control and Supervision to oversee the terms of the agreement, its ability to investigate alleged violations was hindered from the start. Its membership was made up of individuals from Hungary, Poland, Canada, and Indonesia, and it faced a series of challenges that made the organization powerless to stop the violations to the accords. Unfortunately, the Paris Peace Accords did not end the wars in Southeast Asia. On March 18, Lon Nol declared a state of siege for Phnom Penh, as the Khmer Rouge threatened the capital. Only American air power in response to the crisis prevented this from happening. The ability of the United States to respond to similar threats was dealt a significant setback by congressional action.

In 1972, Senators Frank Church (D-Idaho) and Clifford Case (R-New Jersey) introduced an amendment that prohibited continued American military action in Southeast Asia. When Nixon threatened to veto it, the Senate rejected the amendment. It was reintroduced right before the signing of the Paris Peace Accords and approved on June 19, 1973. The Nixon administration worked hard for the amendment's defeat but failed to gain enough support. It passed both houses of Congress with enough votes to make it immune to any veto. The amendment set an August 15 deadline for American military activities in Southeast Asia. It was this amendment that Nixon's successor, Gerald Ford, used as justifi-cation for his lack of action when the North Vietnamese launched their final offensive in late 1974.

Soon after the Case-Church amendment, Congress adopted House Joint Resolution 542, more commonly referred to as the War Powers Resolution, which further reduced the executive's ability to conduct foreign relations without congressional oversight. The resolution required the president to report to Congress within forty-eight hours if he committed US troops to a foreign conflict or significantly increased the number of combat troops in a foreign country. If Congress did not approve the president's decision within sixty days, the troops had to be withdrawn, though a thirty-day extension was possible if the troops' extraction within the sixty-day period might cause casualties. The War Powers Resolution was passed in both houses of Congress on November 7. Even though it was veto-proof, as it had been approved by more than a two-thirds majority, Nixon vetoed it only to have Congress override that veto. It was clear that the mood of the nation was against further ventures into Southeast Asia.

End of the War

Even after the Paris Peace Accords, both the North Vietnamese and the

Building up defenses for the F-12 Delta. DEPARTMENT OF DEFENSE, 64-4852, NARA.

South Vietnamese continued to clash as each side vied for control over the countryside and the people. Each country violated the accords, and both looked to see how the United States would respond. By the end of 1973, it was clear that the United States was out of the war. Congressional actions that year ensured that it would be difficult to reinsert American military power. While the North Vietnamese responded to a series of offensives launched by the Saigon government to reclaim territory that they lost in 1973, they also planned for another offensive to end the conflict and reunite the two Vietnams. The Spring 1975 Offensive was not originally planned to be the final offensive; it was supposed to have come in 1976. However, the initial success of the campaigns coupled with a loss of fighting spirit from some ARVN units accelerated the final collapse of South Vietnam. Attacks in Phuoc Long province to the northeast of Saigon and in the Central Highlands, resulting in the capture of Ban Me Thout, encouraged the North Vietnamese, who also put significant military pressure in I Corps.

When it became clear that the United States would not provide emergency military aid or assistance, Nguyen Van Thieu vacillated between holding ground in the North and regrouping farther to the South. The North Vietnamese had seized the initiative and were pressuring beleaguered ARVN forces whose unit cohesion soon eroded. In March, Nguyen Van Thieu ordered the evacuation of the area north of Danang, which caused a general panic among the populations. Soon both civilian and military personnel vied for any available transportation to get south. While there was a general feeling of confusion and defeat that permeated the South Vietnamese population, there were units that put up a strong defense. The two-week ARVN defense of Xuan Loc in April temporarily slowed the North Vietnamese advance, but the fall of that city ensured that Saigon would be encircled.

As the defense of Xuan Loc ended, President Gerald Ford, who had replaced Nixon after his resignation the previous August, was faced with a decision of whether to come to the aid of the collapsing Republic of Vietnam. Ford's answer came in the form of a speech at Tulane University, where he informed a cheering audience that the United States needed to return to a time before Vietnam and that this would not occur by fighting in a war that was over as far as the United States was concerned. Nguyen Van Thieu had already resigned, but not before he delivered a scathing attack against the United States and its inaction. By the end of April, having encircled Saigon, the North Vietnamese began shelling the capital. On the morning of April 30, the new president, Duong Van Minh, who had replaced Nguyen Van Thieu, ordered his troops to stop fighting. Sixteen minutes later, at 10:40 a.m., US ambassador Graham Martin ordered the final evacuation of American personnel from South Vietnam. Shortly after 12:00 p.m., a North Vietnamese tank penetrated the grounds of the Presidential Palace and accepted the surrender of the Saigon government. Sporadic fighting occurred through May 2, but April 30 marked the end of the Vietnam War and of the Republic of Vietnam.

After the War

The collapse of the South Vietnamese government did not end the suffering of the people in Southeast Asia. Saigon was not the first capital to fall to the Communists in 1975. By 1974, the Khmer Rouge had pushed back the Cambodian army to the major urban centers and a few strategic enclaves throughout the country. It launched its final offensive on January 1, 1975, and ended it on April 17, when the Khmer Rouge captured Phnom Penh. Rather than celebrating an end to its conflict, the Khmer Rouge, under the leadership of Pol Pot, began a campaign to strip Western influence from the country and its people. The new Democratic Kampuchea initiated a genocide that killed approximately three million Cambodians through a combination of execution, forced labor, starvation, and disease. The killings did not end until the newly named Socialist Republic of Vietnam invaded in December 1978. Cambodia's struggles did not end, as those loyal to the old Sihanouk regime battled with Pol Pot followers until 1999. The Cambodian people and economy were devastated from the prolonged fighting. The country remains the poorest in Asia as a result.

In the United States, the aftermath of the Vietnam War haunted US foreign policy. Both Ford and his successor, Jimmy Carter, failed to intervene in Cambodia despite the enormity of the human rights crisis, and the level of hesitation with which it acted in the Middle East and Latin America led to a series of troubled decisions. The United States wanted to forget Vietnam, but, at the same time, it also turned away from those Americans who had been involved in the nearly ten years of combat in Southeast Asia. The Vietnam veteran found little comfort in his or her return to the United States. It was not until the construction and dedication of the Vietnam Veterans Memorial in Washington, D.C., in November 1982 that many veterans began the process of healing from their Vietnam experience.

The sacrifices that American women made were not acknowledged until the November 11, 1993, ceremony, which marked the unveiling of Glenna Goodacre's bronze statue at the Vietnam Veterans Memorial. The Vietnam War remains a significantly contested and debated event in the United States. It changed the nation's society, politics, foreign policy, and people, and while the answers to many questions and concerns that arose from the war continue to be explored and interpreted, the lingering question of "Why Vietnam?" remains.

Suggested Readings

Berman, Larry. *Planning a Tragedy: The Americanization of the War in Vietnam*. New York: Norton, 1982.

Bradley, Mark Philip. *Vietnam at War*. New York: Oxford University Press, 2009.

Buttinger, Joseph. *The Smaller Dragon: A Political History of Vietnam*. New York: Praeger, 1958.

Clodfelter, Michael. *Vietnam in Military Statistics: A History of the Indochina Wars, 1772–1991*. Jefferson, N.C.: McFarland, 1995.

Colby, William, with James McCargar. *Lost Victory*. Chicago: Contemporary Books, 1989.

Dommen, Arthur J. *The Indochinese Experience of the French and the Americans: Nationalism and Communism in Cambodia, Laos, and Vietnam*. Bloomington: Indiana University Press, 2001.

Fall, Bernard. *The Two Viet-Nams*. New York: Praeger, 1964.

Fitzgerald, Frances. *Fire in the Lake: The Vietnamese and the Americans in Vietnam*. New York: Random House, 1972.

Gelb, Leslie H., with Richard K. Betts. *The Irony of Vietnam: The System Worked*. Washington, D.C.: Brookings Institution, 1979.

Gilbert, Marc Jason, ed. *Why the North Won the Vietnam War*. New York: Palgrave, 2002.

Kahin, George McTurnan. *Intervention: How America Became Involved in Vietnam*. New York: Knopf, 1986.

Lawrence, Mark Atwood. *The Vietnam War: A Concise International History*. New York: Oxford University Press, 2008.

Lewy, Guenter. *America in Vietnam*. New York: Oxford University Press, 1978.

Lomperis, Timothy J. *The War Everyone Lost—and Won: America's Intervention in Viet Nam's Twin Struggles*. Baton Rouge: Louisiana State University Press, 1984.

Shaplen, Robert. *The Lost Revolution: The U.S. in Vietnam, 1946–1966*. New York: Harper & Row, 1965.

Smith, Ralph B. *An International History of the Vietnam War*. New York: St. Martin's Press, 1983.

Summers, Harry. *On Strategy: The Vietnam War in Context*. Novato, Calif.: Presidio Press, 1982.